Champlain Valley
MEMORIES
THE EARLY YEARS

ACKNOWLEDGMENTS

The Burlington Free Press is pleased to present *"Champlain Valley Memories ~ The Early Years."*

This unique pictorial book is a publication of the *Burlington Free Press*. However, it is the result of contributions made by many people and organizations from throughout the area.

We are all indebted, first of all, to those early residents of the Champlain Valley who captured their times – our history – in photographs, and provided us with a glimpse into their lives. And, secondly, all valley residents are indebted to the many individuals who are committed to preserving our history in various libraries, archives and personal collections all around the Champlain Valley.

We are pleased to acknowledge the generous contribution of both time and photo archives from the following organizations:

Bixby Memorial Library, Vergennes

Essex Historical Society, Harriett Powell Museum, Essex Junction

Georgia Historical Society, Georgia

Henry Sheldon Museum of Vermont History, Stewart-Swift Research Center, Middlebury

Huntington Historical Community Trust, Huntington

St. Albans Historical Society, St. Albans

University of Vermont, Bailey/Howe Library, Burlington

Published by Pediment Publishing, a division of The Pediment Group, Inc. www.pediment.com   Printed in Canada

Table of Contents

FOREWORD

There are many who will claim their piece of the world is unique, but we who live in the Champlain Valley know that living in Vermont is special. Our great lake, our mountains, our farms and our beautiful towns have forged the bonds that make us Vermonters. We bask in all-too-short summers. We revel in the long winters. We endure the flies and mud. We would exchange our lifestyles – and our heritage – with no one. Our landscape can still tell us much of the trials and joys that our forefathers experienced in scratching a living from this difficult but beautiful place.

Each day for the past 176 years, the *Burlington Free Press* has chronicled life here in the Champlain Valley. That is why we felt it was entirely appropriate that we bring to you this collection of photographs that capture slices of time when life was simpler – and more difficult – a time when many of the values we treasure as Vermonters were born.

With the cooperation of many of the area's historical societies and libraries we bring you a glimpse of life in the Champlain Valley from the 1860s to the 1930s. Enjoy Vermonters working, playing, celebrating and pulling together in times of need.

We are pleased to donate the proceeds from this book to our Newspapers in Education Program. Through this program we bring the newspaper, free of charge, to many classrooms in area schools. We earnestly hope that by gaining a better understanding of local, national and international events our children will understand their places in the next generation of Vermonters and better lead us into the future.

We at the *Burlington Free Press* are happy to publish *Champlain Valley Memories – The Early Years* for your enjoyment. We are pleased to step back from the frenzied pace of bringing the news to your home every day and reflect upon our common past. We hope you enjoy this collection as much as we do.

James M. Carey
President and Publisher
Burlington Free Press

VIEWS OF THE VALLEY

The Champlain Valley in the 1800s was farm country. Most people lived on the farm; they had a cow or two, chickens, pigs; they grew oats and wheat and hay. The bigger farms raised sheep for wool – cows would get their turn in the early 1900s.

Eighty percent of the state was open farmland; the best land was in the Valley and went for $10 an acre. Nestled close to the lake and between the Adirondacks and the Green Mountains, the Champlain Valley soil was rich with nutrients. Horses provided the power for Valley farms: They were hitched to wagons and sleighs and plows; they pulled logs out of the woods and rode treadmills to thresh oats.

Life was different at the turn of the century: men and women used separate entrances at the Burlington Post Office. Women were not allowed to vote at town meeting. Most babies were born at home and one in eight died before its first birthday. Life expectancy was 49 years. A fine Burlington eight-room house could be had for $3,400.

Kerosene lamps were ubiquitous; electricity was found only in the biggest towns. A trip to town took hours and was only undertaken out of necessity. To travel further, people took the stagecoach or train. Lake Champlain was still a primary commercial route for Vermont; it was the avenue down which Vermonters exported their wool and canned goods and lumber and furniture and cloth and stone work.

At the turn of the century, Vermont had its time in the limelight as well: Lila Vanderbilt Webb purchased the farms that became Shelburne Farm, a place where, for decades, presidents and dignitaries were entertained. Admiral George Dewey, a Vermont native, became the hero of the Spanish-American War.

Main Street, Bristol, circa 1870. *Courtesy Henry Sheldon Museum of Vermont History*

View of Burlington at Church Street, circa 1860. *Courtesy Burlington photo file, UVM*

Main Street, looking south, Middlebury, 1880s. *Courtesy Henry Sheldon Museum of Vermont History*

Main Street looking north, Middlebury, 1880s. The second building on the right with the dormer window is Pine Hall, once the Frank Bond skating rink. *Courtesy Henry Sheldon Museum of Vermont History*

Main Street, St. Albans, 1880. *Courtesy St. Albans Historical Society*

A view of Georgia June 28, 1887 showing the Georgia High Bridge with wooden sides. *Courtesy Georgia Historical Society*

College Street, Burlington, circa 1879. *Courtesy Burlington photo file, UVM*

Main Street looking northeast, Vergennes, circa 1892. *Courtesy Bixby Memorial Library*

Main Street, Middlebury, 1890s. *Courtesy Henry Sheldon Museum of Vermont History*

Brainerd Block (corner of Bank and Main streets), St. Albans, circa 1890. *Courtesy St. Albans Historical Society*

Main Street, Vergennes, circa 1892. *Courtesy Bixby Memorial Library*

Street scene in downtown Bristol, late 1800s. *Photo courtesy General Photo Collection, UVM*

View of Bristol Notch, 1892. *Courtesy Henry Sheldon Museum of Vermont History*

View of the New Haven River, 1892. *Courtesy Henry Sheldon Museum of Vermont History*

Snowy street scene in Burlington, late 1800s. *Courtesy Burlington photo file, UVM*

View of Otter Creek Falls, 1893. *Courtesy Bixby Memorial Library*

View down Main Street looking west, from the tower of the Episcopal Church, Vergennes, 1893.
Courtesy Bixby Memorial Library

View of Church Street, Burlington, circa 1895. *Courtesy Burlington photo file, UVM*

Church Street, Burlington, circa 1895. *Courtesy Burlington photo file, UVM*

Street scene, St. Albans, early 1900s. The billboards are advertising Pawnee Wild West Shows. *Courtesy St. Albans Historical Society*

Boat landing at Burlington, early 1900s. Champlain Transportation Company Wharf and general offices, Shepard and Morse Lumber Company, Champlain Yacht Club and the old railroad station can be seen in the distance. *Courtesy Burlington photo file, UVM*

Burlington Harbor, early 1900s. *Courtesy Burlington photo file, UVM*

Burlington Harbor, early 1900s. The steamboat Chateaugay is on the right. *Courtesy Burlington photo file, UVM*

View of Winooski, early 1900s.
Courtesy L.L. McAllister collection, UVM

North Main Street, St. Albans, 1901. *Photo courtesy St. Albans Historical Society*

College Street, Burlington, circa 1900. *Photo courtesy Burlington photo file, UVM*

Covered bridge over Halpin Falls, Middlebury. *Courtesy Henry Sheldon Museum of Vermont History*

The Common, Memorial Hall in the distance, Essex, circa 1910. *Courtesy Essex Historical Society, Harriett Powell Museum*

Brownell Block, Essex Junction, circa 1910.
Courtesy Essex Historical Society, Harriett Powell Museum

Brooklyn Street (now Bridge Street), looking east, Huntington, circa 1910.
Courtesy Huntington Historical Community Trust, Lorraine Jones collection

A view of Jericho Center, circa 1910. *Courtesy Clinton M. Russell, Jr. and Barbara Mudgett-Russell*

People gather in downtown Winooski to watch the 10th Cavalry ride through town, circa 1916.

Photo courtesy General Photo Collection, UVM

Lake Street, looking west, St. Albans, 1920.

Courtesy St. Albans Historical Society

Church Street looking toward the church, July, 1931. *Courtesy L.L. McAllister collection, UVM*

Main Street, looking south at the foot of Congress Street, August 12, 1937 in St. Albans.

Courtesy St. Albans Historical Society

Main Street, St. Albans, circa 1925. *Photo courtesy St. Albans Historical Society*

Pearl Street, Burlington, April 23, 1934. *Courtesy L.L. McAllister collection, UVM*

EDUCATION

Public education in Vermont's Champlain Valley was largely a local affair in the 1800s and early 1900s. Most schools were one-room schoolhouses with children ages 8 through 15 getting their learning from one teacher. Only three years of education were required. By the early 1900s, Vermont had 1,400 one-room schools and 300 multi-room schools.

A shift to more state control began in 1915, as a result of a respected study that rebuked Vermont for teachers that lacked training, curriculums that had little substance and schoolhouses that were in dilapidated. The state provided additional money, extended the school year from 30 to 34 weeks and began oversight of basic curriculum. This trend has continued to today when the state oversees school financing to ensure equality in the quality of instruction.

In higher education, the Valley has had several distinctions. The University of Vermont, founded in 1791, is the fifth oldest university in New England. It also was the first university to admit women and African-Americans into Phi Beta Kappa honor society. Middlebury College, meanwhile, was founded in 1800 by a handful of energetic townspeople; it was first intended as a training college for ministers. In 1823, Alexander Twilight graduated from Middlebury College, the first African American citizen to earn a baccalaureate degree at an American college.

Middlebury Graded School, circa 1902. *Courtesy Henry Sheldon Museum of Vermont History*

Burlington High School graduating class of 1891. *Courtesy Burlington photo file, UVM*

College group on the stairs of the Old Chapel, Middlebury College, circa 1890. *Courtesy Henry Sheldon Museum of Vermont History*

Old Chapel at Middlebury College, 1890s. *Courtesy Henry Sheldon Museum of Vermont History*

Florence Allen studies in her room at Middlebury College, late 1800s. *Courtesy Henry Sheldon Museum of Vermont History*

Vergennes High School students and faculty, circa 1893. *Courtesy Bixby Memorial Library*

Franklin Grammar School students, St. Albans, 1890s.
Courtesy St. Albans Historical Society

First girls building of the Vermont Reformed School in Vergennes, late 1800s. The building later housed Weeks School and then the Industrial School. Originally the building served as the officers quarters of the U.S. Arsenal. *Courtesy Bixby Memorial Library*

Newton Academy, Shoreham, circa 1898. *Courtesy Henry Sheldon Museum of Vermont History*

Classical Institute graduating class, 1897. First row: Emma Monta, Ellen McNall, Pearlie Gilmore, Lora Wheeler, Stanley Tuttle, Mary Leach, Mary Farrand. Second row: Mirra Monta, Anna Lane, Caleb Pillsbury, Lila Whipple, Florence Stater. *Courtesy Essex Historical Society, Harriett Powell Museum*

Children in front of their school, School District No. 3, Huntington. Fred B. Blodgett was the teacher. Those in the photo are: Clara S. Cutter, Edith I. Collins, Fred Cota, James Durand, Bennie Durand, Walter Durand, Bertha L. Dartt, Grace Franklin, Gertie Franklin, Nellie E. Fargo, Vernon H. Fargo, Robert S. Johnson, Gladys F. Johnson, Daisy M. Kenyon, Ella S. Kenyon, Clarence L. Kenyon, Earl C. Morrill, Julia H. Morrill, Forest M. Norton, Greta W. Norton, Ira H. Ring, Jane E. Ring, Howard J. Ring, Inza M. Ring, Elbridge W. Ross, Eula I. Scofield, Abbie B. Scofield, Rudie R. Scofield, Herbert J. Stevens, Orvis B. Stevens, Eleanor E. Sweet, Myrtle E. Swinger, Fred J. Salvas, Paul L. Salvas, Henry Sears, Willie Sears, Kate D. Tompson, Polly J. Warren.

Courtesy Huntington Historical Community Trust, Lorraine Jones collection

Pomeroy School children, early 1900s. *Photo courtesy Burlington photo file, UVM*

These gentlemen are thought to be Middlebury College students, circa 1900. *Courtesy Henry Sheldon Museum of Vermont History*

Vergennes High School graduates, 1899. *Courtesy Bixby Memorial Library*

Pomeroy School children, early 1900s. *Courtesy Burlington photo file, UVM*

Students in front of the Classical Institute, Essex, circa 1900. *Courtesy Essex Historical Society, Harriett Powell Museum*

Burlington High School on the northwest corner of College and South Willard. *Courtesy Burlington photo file, UVM*

"Old Home Day" at Beeman Academy, New Haven, early 1900s. *Courtesy Henry Sheldon Museum of Vermont History*

Catherine E. Ross School, early 1900s. *Courtesy Huntington Historical Community Trust, Lorraine Jones collection*

Stone School on Polly Hubbard Road, 1905.
Courtesy Georgia Historical Society

Breadloaf School (Ripton), students, circa 1908. Left to right, back row: Mary Tierney, Jim Tierney, Ray Boynton, Robson Atwood. Second row: Robert Noble, Albert Fletcher, Oliata Fletcher. Front row: Isabell Noble, George Tierney, Edna Kirby, Victor Boynton, unidentified, Ida Boynton. *Courtesy Henry Sheldon Museum of Vermont History*

Brick School children, 1919. First row: June Constantine, Mary Hurlbut, Charles Ballard, Bertha Pattee, Arthella Reynolds, Doris Dufresne, Edith Pattee, Lennie Perry, Sally Dufresne. Second row: Teacher Sadie Wilbur, Kenneth Bevins, Mike Loomis, John Cleveland, Walter Perry (in front of Charlotte Loomis), Kermit Webster, Wayne Bevins, Ruth Ballard. Third Row: Aldis Martin, Kenneth Webster, Eunice Dunton, Charlotte Loomis, Roy Hurlbut, Robert Cameron, Harold Cameron, Eldan Reynolds, Homer Lambert. *Courtesy Georgia Historical Society*

First graduating class of the new Essex Junction High School on Prospect Street, 1913. *Courtesy Essex Historical Society, Harriett Powell Museum*

West Georgia School students, 1906. Back row: Florence Boyden, Carolyn Warren and teacher, Lulu Warren, John Duffy, Elmer Decker, Elmer Gaboree. Second row: Vernon Duffy, Curtis Bevins, Stearns Boyden, Clayton Gaboree, Clinton Barrows. First row: Lila Gaboree, Mildred Barrows, Beatrice Bevins, Helen Mahoney, Nel Boyden, Nellie Wood, Henry Boyden.

Courtesy Georgia Historical Society

Miltonboro School students, 1919. Leslie Elmore, Dora Cameron, Carleton Richards, Donald Duquette, Bertha Cameron, Lillian Richards, Laura Underwood, Elsie Duquette, Etta Underwood, Mary Cameron, Elmer Bullock, Clifton Elmer, Herman Hibbard. *Courtesy Georgia Historical Society*

Georgia Plains School. Left to right, back row: Eugene Ballard, William Sartwell, Carlton Blake, Leon Cross, Arthur Cota, Ruth Green, Gertrude Cross, Ruby Tatro, Bertha Wood. Front row: Merle Wood, Harold Cota, Donald Wood, Allen Pierce, Lynford Tatro, Clarence Cross, the rest are unidentified as well as the entire middle row. *Courtesy Georgia Historical Society*

Vergennes grade fourth grade children, 1920. First row: Kenneth Sorrell, Ruby Hamel, Augusta Hack, Esther Blair, Ralph Ryan, Donald Fraser, Donald Laramie, Louis Langvin, Marion Judoin, Florence Dugan. Second row: Donald Little, Cecil Clark, Howard Sessions, Onslow Brown, Ruth Gowett, Miner Milo, Malcolm Benton, Kenneth Larrow. Third row: Malcolm Mulholland, Mabel Moses, Gretchen Fanslow, Catherine VanKeuran, George Barton, George Rose, Frederick Krampitz, Ruth Barton. *Courtesy Bixby Memorial Library*

Senior play members from St. Albans High School, 1921. Left to right, back row: Alden Miller, Hortense Beeman, Wesley Sanborn, Catherine McGinn, Bradley Soule, Dorothy Hefflon, James Walsh. Front row: Henry Greene, Laura Catlin, Edward Rousseau, Bernadette Mayo, Edward Twohey. *Courtesy St. Albans Historical Society*

Nazareth School class, Burlington, 1931. *Courtesy Burlington photo file, UVM*

Students in front of the Catherine E. Ross School, early 1932. *Courtesy Huntington Historical Community Trust, Lorraine Jones collection*

Community gathering at Bellows Free Academy, Fairfax, circa 1928. *Photo courtesy General Photo Collection, UVM*

Book wagon stops at Skunk Hill School, circa 1935. *Courtesy Georgia Historical Society*

Graduating seniors at Bellows Free Academy in Fairfax, June 1926. *Courtesy Georgia Historical Society*

COMMERCE

For much of its early years, the Champlain Valley's commerce was tied to big industry or farming. Industry in the Valley were the big employers. Business sprang up to support them, supplying them with materials or supplying their workers with what was needed to live.

But farming was the predominate way of life throughout the Valley, particularly in Franklin and Addison counties. Commerce consisted of farm support: dry goods stores, grain and equipment dealers, tractor and farm equipment salesmen, dairies, harness shops, blacksmiths and wool merchants.

The late 1800s and early 1900s brought a new type of commerce to the Valley – tourism. People from afar arrived by train and/or ferry and stayed at gargantuan hotels; often the same company owned all three. The hotels offered majestic views of the lake and mountains and an opportunity for people to take a deep breath and relax. Growing prosperity in the Valley brought the need for a wider range of retail goods, from drugs to fruits, hardware to fire insurance, from candy to oil.

Dodge-Plymouth dealership on North Avenue, Burlington, 1935. *Courtesy L.L. McAllister collection, UVM*

Stevens House Hotel, Vergennes, late 1800s.

Courtesy Bixby Memorial Library

Addison
House,
Middlebury,
circa 1870.

*Courtesy The
Sheldon
Museum*

Lake Dunmore Hotel, Salisbury, circa 1875. *Courtesy Henry Sheldon Museum of Vermont History*

Interior of William H. Sheldon's store, Middlebury, circa 1890. *Courtesy Henry Sheldon Museum of Vermont History*

Businesses at the southwest corner of Church and Main streets, Burlington. 1880s. *Courtesy Burlington photo file, UVM*

Eldred Drug Store at the southeast corner of Kingman and Federal Streets, St. Albans, 1893. *Courtesy St. Albans Historical Society*

Benedict Store, Middlebury, circa 1894. Standing in front: Ranson Benedict, proprietor and John W. Wright, clerk. *Courtesy Henry Sheldon Museum of Vermont History*

Business on the corner of Kingman and Main streets, St. Albans, late 1800s. *Courtesy St. Albans Historical Society*

C.H. Morton and other businesses in St. Albans, late 1800s. *Courtesy St. Albans Historical Society*

Stinehour's Hotel, Highgate, late 1800s. *Courtesy St. Albans Historical Society*

Burlington Grocery Company, early 1900s. *Courtesy Burlington photo file, UVM*

Congress Hall Hotel in Sheldon Springs, late 1800s. *Courtesy St. Albans Historical Society*

Ralph Oscar Mudgett family in front of the R.O. Mudgett and Company store.

Courtesy Barbara Mudgett-Russell

H.B. Slack grocery store and meat market, Vergennes, circa 1900. *Courtesy Bixby Memorial Library*

Harness shop on Merchants Row, Middlebury, circa 1900. *Courtesy Henry Sheldon Museum of Vermont History*

Reed & Patrick's store in Hinesburg, early 1900s. *Courtesy General Photo Collection, UVM*

Interior of Benedict's Store, 5 Merchants Row, Middlebury, circa 1903. Those in the photo: Ranson Benedict, Prop; Hazel Signer, clerk; Eugene J. Shambo, clerk; Albert W. Kirkland, clerk; Napoleon J. Beudrean, clerk; unidentified customer; George Dwine, cellar-man; Joseph B. Cobb, band leader and customer, Mrs. Nelson Signer, customer. *Courtesy Henry Sheldon Museum of Vermont History*

Isaac Sterns Drug Store, Middlebury, circa 1905. Left to right: Carl Stern (Middlebury College class of 1914, lost his life in World War I), Dr. Stern and ____ Comstock. *Courtesy Henry Sheldon Museum of Vermont History*

J. Calvi and Company Fruit and Confectionery store, Main Street, Middlebury, 1902. *Courtesy Henry Sheldon Museum of Vermont History*

Hotel, Sayles General Store and Post Office on Brooklyn Street (now Bridge Street), Huntington, circa 1905. *Courtesy Huntington Historical Community Trust*

Benedict's horse-drawn delivery wagon in front of the business on Merchants Row, Middlebury, circa 1903. *Courtesy Henry Sheldon Museum of Vermont History*

Interior of the E.P. Cushman and Son Dry Good Store on Merchants Row in the Battell Block, Middlebury, circa 1910. Edward Pinney Cushman, who founded the store in 1883, is on the left; his son Harry Leon Cushman is on the right. The store continued in business at the Merchants Row location until about 1934, when it was moved around the corner on 47 Main Street. The seats in the left counter area were for the comfort of the customers examining the yard goods. *Courtesy Henry Sheldon Museum of Vermont History*

Interior of R.S. Benedict's Store at 5 Merchants' Row, Middlebury, circa 1915. Left to right, Ranson S. Benedict, owner; Gertrude Hill, bookkeeper; Stanley Vancellette, clerk. *Courtesy Henry Sheldon Museum of Vermont History*

Exterior of a store owned by Mr. Herrick, Vergennes, early 1900s. *Courtesy Bixby Memorial Library*

John H. Stewart inside his hardware store on Merchants Row, Middlebury, circa 1918. *Courtesy Henry Sheldon Museum of Vermont History*

Exterior of the Free Press Printing Company. *Courtesy Burlington photo file, UVM*

Socony Gas Station, Burlington, 1920s. *Courtesy L.L. McAllister collection, UVM*

Composing room,
Free Press Printing
Company, Burlington.
Courtesy Burlington photo
file, UVM

Norton and Ellis general store owned by Ernest Norton, Huntington, 1920s. There was an apartment upstairs. *Courtesy Huntington Historical Community Trust, Lorraine Jones collection*

Interior of Haven's Clothing Store, Vergennes, 1930s. *Courtesy Bixby Memorial Library*

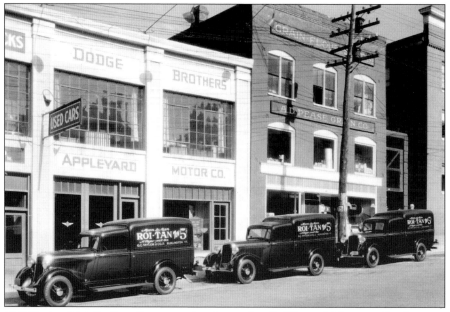

O.C. Taylor Distributing Company trucks on South Winooski Avenue, Burlington, 1933. *Courtesy L.L. McAllister collection, UVM*

Meat market at the First National Store, Burlington, circa 1935. *Courtesy L.L. McAllister collection, UVM*

Interior of the Montgomery Store, 1930s. *Courtesy Burlington photo file, UVM*

Exterior of the First National Stores, Burlington, circa 1935. *Courtesy L.L. McAllister collection, UVM*

Interior of the First National Store, Burlington, circa 1935. *Courtesy L.L. McAllister collection, UVM*

Green Mountain Oil Company and vehicles, St. Albans, 1939. *Courtesy St. Albans Historical Society*

INDUSTRY

Industry congregated on the three major rivers that run from the Green Mountains into Lake Champlain: the Lamoille River, the Winooski River and Otter Creek. Textile mills, lumber mills, wood manufacturing factories, machining factories were at their strongest from the late 1800s through the early 1900s.

The largest of the factory centers was in Winooski where, at one time, American Woolen employed 2,600 workers and was by far the largest employer in the state. In the early 1940s, 60 percent of the employees were women and almost one-third were immigrants.

Vermont's industry offered people an opportunity to get off the farm, but what was offered was often low wages, no benefits and tough conditions. Vermont also employed many children in its mills in the early 1800s. In 1867, the state became the last state to enact a law restricting child labor.

The textile jobs eventually shut down, taking the machinery – and the jobs – to the deep south where the cost of doing business was less. As with the rest of the country, manufacturing now provides less than 25 percent of all of Vermont's jobs.

Shelburne Shipyard, circa 1920. *Courtesy General Photo Collection, UVM*

Early arrivals inspecting the new vessel
at the Shelburne Harbor Shipyard.
Courtesy General Photo Collection, UVM

Stone Cotton Factory before the November 22, 1891 fire.
This factory was built in 1811. In 1817, Joseph Gordon
came from Scotland and built 20 power looms which
are believed to have been some of the first power looms
built in the United States. In 1820, the building contained
840 spindles for cotton, 15 power looms together with
two wool-carding machines. The spindles produced a
sufficient quantity of yarn daily for 500 yards of sheeting.
Courtesy Henry Sheldon Museum of Vermont History

Industrial area at the falls at stone pier bridge, Main Street, Middlebury, circa 1885. *Courtesy Henry Sheldon Museum of Vermont History*

Men stand on the old shed roof at Lincoln Center Mill, circa 1885. *Courtesy Henry*
Sheldon Museum of Vermont History

Drury brickyard. This was a major industry in the Essex Junction area, late 1800s.
Courtesy Essex Historical Society, Harriett Powell Museum

American Woolen Company dyeing room employees, Winooski, circa 1900. *Cour-*
tesy L.L. McAllister collection, UVM

Old Huntley Saw Mill and butter tub factory, Ripton, circa 1900. *Courtesy Henry Shel-*
don Museum of Vermont History

Canning factory at Park and Maple streets, Essex Junction, early 1900s. Farmers would bring their crops to this plant to have their vegetables canned. *Courtesy Essex Historical Society, Harriett Powell Museum*

Norton's Grist Mill, Vergennes, early 1900s.

Courtesy Bixby Memorial Library

The Georgia Coop Creamery in 1934. This was a milk drop station for the Milton Coop Creamery. *Courtesy Georgia Historical Society*

Steamer "Ticonderoga" in dry-dock at Shelburne Harbor, October 1929. *Courtesy General Photo Collection, UVM*

Steamer "Ticonderoga" in dry-dock at Shelburne Harbor, circa 1920. *Courtesy General Photo Collection, UVM*

Central plant of the Burlington Street Department on Pine Street, 1934. *Courtesy L.L. McAllister collection, UVM*

The "Legonia" at the dock, Burlington, January 9, 1934. *Courtesy L.L. McAllister collection, UVM*

HOME & FARM

In the early 1800s, the Champlain Valley was known around the world as the epicenter of the sheep industry and was the world's major provider of wool. The region was known for its purebred Spanish Merino breed. All this changed as competition – and dropping wool prices – drove Vermont farmers to sell off their sheep and get into the cow dairy business.

Vermont had a sizable butter business by the early 1900s, supplying New York and Boston with its finest butter. Improved technologies in the 1930s – the more widespread use of electricity – brought an increase in milk and cheese production.

In the late 1800s most people lived on a small, subsistence farm. At one time, Vermont had over 33,000 farms. The Valley held the best soils – lots of nutrients and clay left over after the Ice Age glaciers retreated – and these turned out to be perfect for hay and grains.

The small farms were family businesses with everyone contributing; chores were many and hours were long. Vermonters began leaving farming in the 1860s, after the Civil War, when soldiers discovered land in other parts of the country that were less hilly and rocky and far more productive. Those that stayed in Vermont did everything they could to keep going from growing feed to chickens to making sure there were plenty of sap buckets up in the spring for the cash crop – maple syrup.

Threshing oats on the Chapin Farm, Essex, circa 1910. *Courtesy Essex Historical Society, Harriett Powell Museum*

Holland Weeks Homestead, Salisbury, 1872. *Courtesy Henry Sheldon Museum of Vermont History*

Holcomb Place, Starksboro, circa 1875. Samuel D. and Cynthia Holcomb are in the carriage. *Courtesy Henry Sheldon Museum of Vermont History*

Residence of the D. Hubbard family, New Haven, circa 1877. *Courtesy Henry Sheldon Museum of Vermont History*

Cartwells residence, Weybridge, late 1800s. *Courtesy Henry Sheldon Museum of Vermont History*

Farm house in Weybridge, circa 1890.
Courtesy Henry Sheldon Museum of Vermont History

James family home, Shoreham, circa 1890. *Courtesy Henry Sheldon Museum of Vermont History*

Hyde residence owned by Alfred and Caroline Fuller Hyde, 1882. Their three daughters from left: Bertha Amelia, Juliette and Annie Armanda. *Courtesy Georgia Historical Society*

Worthington C. Smith house, St. Albans, late 1800s. *Courtesy St. Albans Historical Society*

W.B. Johnson Mill and Creamery (formerly Butler Grist Mill) on the Winooski River, 1893. *Courtesy Essex Historical Society, Harriett Powell Museum*

Maple sugaring operation, late 1800s. *Courtesy General Photo Collection, UVM*

Woman stands next to the trees of her maple sugaring harvest. *Courtesy General Photo Collection, UVM*

Maple sugaring operation, late 1800s. *Courtesy General Photo Collection, UVM*

Wagons piled high with hay, South Winooski Avenue, Burlington, late 1800s. *Courtesy Burlington photo file, UVM*

House located at 47 Prospect Street in Burlington, late 1800s. *Courtesy Burlington photo file, UVM*

Mrs. G.E. Linsley Cedar Beach cottage in Charlotte, late 1800s. *Courtesy General Photo Collection, UVM*

Doolittle-Crane House on the corner of Bank and Pine streets, Burlington, late 1800s. *Courtesy Burlington photo file, UVM*

Picking strawberries at McNeil's farm, New Haven, circa 1898. *Courtesy Bixby Memorial Library*

Haying scene at "The Point Farm" owned by Gov. J. Gregory Smith, St. Albans. *Courtesy St. Albans Historical Society*

Nells house on Main Street, Burlington.
Courtesy Burlington photo file, UVM

Old Judge Fish home, Vergennes, July 3, 1909. This was the day of the Champlain Tercentenary celebration. *Courtesy Bixby Memorial Library*

Dr. Arkley in front of his house and office at 64 Main Street, Essex Junction, early 1900s. *Courtesy Barbara Mudgett-Russell*

Burley's pose in front of their home on Hinesburg Road, Monkton, circa 1910. Mr. Henry Lyman Burley, Mrs. Alice (Carpenter) Burley, daughters, Sadie and Agnes. *Courtesy Henry Sheldon Museum of Vermont History*

Antoine Carpenter sitting in front of his home with four unknown people, Monkton Ridge, circa 1910. *Courtesy Henry Sheldon Museum of Vermont History*

Jericho Center residential area, circa 1915. *Courtesy Clinton M. Russell, Jr. and Barbara Mudgett-Russell*

International Harvester tractors on display in St. Albans, circa 1920.
Courtesy St. Albans Historical Society

SOCIETY

In the early days of Champlain Valley the work days were long and arduous. Social time was rare and was usually spent at a neighbors or a barn dance. Sunday's were different.

In the Valley there were several distinct groups of church-goers.

To the north, in Franklin County, most settlers were Catholic – French-Canadian mostly – and churches were grand and made of stone or brick. In the south, in Addison County, most were Protestant – mostly from Europe. Churches were often made of wood and simpler in nature. Burlington had some of the region's largest and more ornate churches.

Church was one of the few times that those living a relatively solitary life could see their neighbors and friends. A hundred years ago, religious observances were a much stronger part of life.

There were other social outlets in the Valley. Granges were big, each boasting hundreds of members for what was largely a farm organization. Other social organizations included the Masons and town bands. Many towns also had an "opera" house, though it was a rare time when a diva would actually be on stage. Often the shows were male-only burlesques; the "opera house" title gave them a respectability.

In 1893, a social event, "Kirmess" was held at the Opera House in Burlington. The production ran from December 2-9 and involved 250 adults and children. This group was called "On the Bowery." In the photo: Ed Farrar, Sam Huntington, Charlie Mower, Fred Mitchell, Geo. Briggs, Edwin B. Allen, F.W. Hewes, Archie Bradford. *Courtesy Burlington photo file, UVM*

Congregational Church, Middlebury, 1891. *Courtesy Henry Sheldon Museum of Vermont History*

Middlebury Band members, circa 1870. *Courtesy Henry Sheldon Museum of Vermont History*

Grange Council members assembled in front of the Addison Town Hall, 1875. *Courtesy Henry Sheldon Museum of Vermont History*

Salisbury Congregational Sunday School, September 28, 1885. Those in the photo include: John Lamorder, Dick Kelsey, Bessie Thomas, Bessie Bump, Bernice Thomas, Mable Smead, Jennie Kendall, Florence Ellis, Etta Kelsey, Carrie Grace, Winnie Bly, Artie Bump, Mrs. D. Ingalls, Minnie Mack, Will Lamorder, John Mack, Clarence Smead, Denny Cloyes, Archie Sheldon, Lena Young, Ida Thomas, Hattie Kendall, Carrie Severy, Allie Wainwright, Hattie Henderson, Fred Cloyes, Winona Dean, Fred Sumner, Mrs. O.M. Bump, Fred Cobb, Mrs. Mary Dean, Frank Bump, Dr. O.M. Bump, Mrs. Ida Martin, Mrs. C.A. Bump, Mrs. Cora Thomas, Fred Hamilton, Cyrus Bump, Dean Horace Sheldon, Lottie Conant, Mrs. L.N. Waterhouse, Laura Severy, Carrie Thomas, Mrs. F.A. Dyer, Mrs. Ben Eastwood, Mrs. Dan Westcott, Mrs. Esther Wainwright, Mrs. Jennie Cloyes, Mrs. John Cloyes, Mrs. O. Nelson, Mrs. E.A. Hamilton, Mrs. Horace Sheldon, Mrs. D.B. Kingsley, Lew Bump, Mrs. A.A. Smead, Stella Kelsey, Cora Kingsley, Chet Kingsley, David Ingalls, Mrs. Jas Thomas, Mrs. John Race, Benj. Eastwood, Ed Thomas, A.A. Smead, Orrin Nelson, John E. Weeks, Dan Westcott, Dennie B. Kingsley, John Cloyes, Will Bump, Rev. Mr. Geddings, N.A. Gibbs, Col. E.A. Hamilton, Geo. D. Merriam, L.N. Waterhouse. *Courtesy Henry Sheldon Museum of Vermont History*

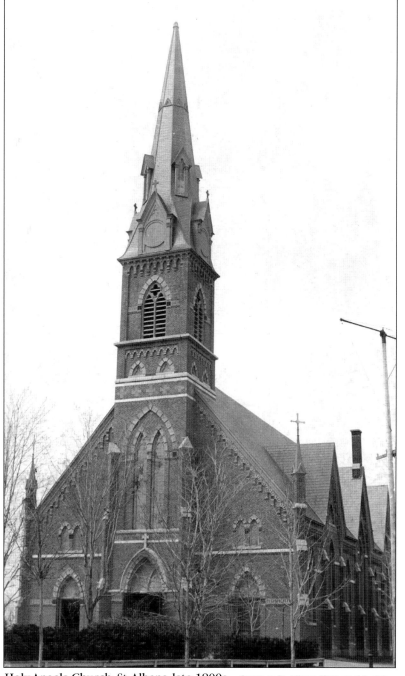

Holy Angels Church, St. Albans, late 1800s. *Courtesy St. Albans Historical Society*

Rev. Charles W. Clark speaking at the Congregational Church in Georgia Center, late 1800s. *Courtesy General Photo Collection, UVM*

In 1893, a social event, "Kirmess" was held at the Opera House in Burlington. The production ran from December 2-9 and involved 250 adults and children. This group of children were known as "Blossoms." In the photo: Lilly Barrows, Kathleen Allen, Stella Moulton, Grace Russell, Nellie Hendee, Florence Russell, Nellie Johns, Hortense Griffin, Katie Hickok, Mary Hickok, Stella Coutermash, Harold Gates, Robert Owen, Willie Walker, Willis Hill, Frank Chamberlin, Arthur Tyndall, Walter Belrose, Harry Hicks, Arthur Pope, Morton Davis, Ralph Kendall and John Wright. *Courtesy Burlington photo file, UVM*

Burlington Unitarian Church, early 1900s. *Photo courtesy Burlington photo file, UVM*

Vergennes Baptist Church, early 1900s. The church burned in 1929, *Courtesy Bixby Memorial Library*

Vergennes City Band, late 1800s. *Courtesy Bixby Memorial Library*

Church group in front of the Baptist Church in Bristol, early 1900s. *Courtesy Henry Sheldon Museum of Vermont History*

Georgia Cornet Band, Fairfax, 1902. *Courtesy Georgia Historical Society*

Trinity Church, Milton, circa 1905. *Courtesy St. Albans Historical Society*

Baptist Church and parsonage, Huntington, circa 1905. It was built in 1870. *Courtesy Huntington Historical Community Trust*

B'Nai Brith fifth anniversary banquet at Joseph Frank Lodge No. 1109, Burlington, January 22, 1933. *Courtesy L.L. McAllister collection, UVM*

St. Paul's Church, Burlington.
Photo courtesy Burlington photo file, UVM

Sherman's Military Band, Burlington, circa 1920.
Courtesy Burlington photo file, UVM

St. Albans School boys band, circa 1934. *Courtesy Georgia Historical Society*

Interior of St. Paul's Church, Burlington. *Courtesy Burlington photo file, UVM*

Round Church in Richmond, circa 1939. *Photo courtesy General Photo Collection, UVM*

RECREATION

Sports played a significant role in community life in towns in the Champlain Valley. Public schools began supporting boys' athletic teams in the late 1800s with girls' teams taking hold in the early 1900s.

Vermont college teams have produced many great athletes, including several who went on to have successful professional baseball and hockey careers. Burlington's first professional baseball team was formed in 1903 for the princely sum of $3,000. Games were played on Centennial Field near the University of Vermont. The team was a success in large part because of the region's love of the game: Schools had baseball teams, neighborhoods had baseball teams and even the mills had baseball teams.

Much of modern-day American skiing owes its origins to Vermont and its invention of the ski lift. Today's famous Vermont ski areas, many of which look out over the Champlain Valley, produced many winter Olympians in the last century.

For recreational activities, the Champlain Valley has long offered boating, sailing, canoeing, skiing, sled dog racing, fishing, hunting and hiking. Lake Champlain has drawn tourists for more than a century and, in the winter, Burlington's Winter Carnival long attracted hardy souls from all over.

St. Albans High School football team, 1919. *Courtesy St. Albans Historical Society*

Enjoying an afternoon on the river in Ferrisburg Center, circa 1887. *Courtesy Bixby Memorial Library*

Boating party at Lake Dunmore, circa 1890. *Courtesy Henry Sheldon Museum of Vermont History*

Ice boating, Burlington, circa 1886. *Courtesy Burlington photo file, UVM*

Boating at Otter Creek Falls, Vergennes, late 1800s. *Courtesy Bixby Memorial Library*

Middlebury College Baseball Team, 1890. I. Ross, Captain; H. Owen; A.A. Livery; B.F. Wynne; E. Cleft; J. Hollister; E Bryant; I. Taylor; P Ross; F. Seeley. *Courtesy Henry Sheldon Museum of Vermont History*

Addison County Fair Grounds, late 1800s. *Courtesy Henry Sheldon Museum of Vermont History*

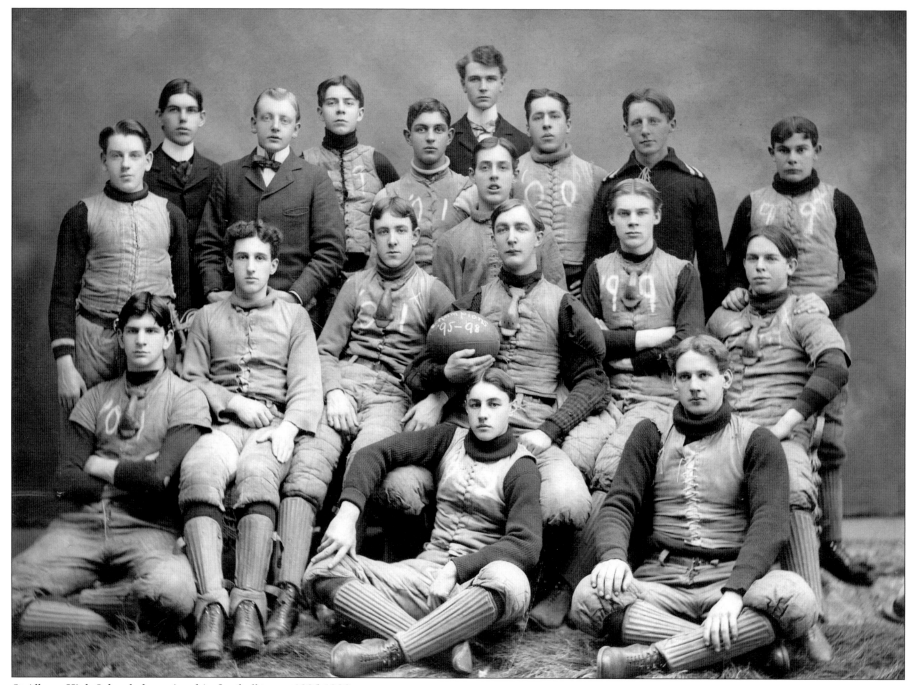

St. Albans High School championship football team, 1895-1898.   *Courtesy St. Albans Historical Society*

Boating on Lake Dunmore, circa 1900. *Courtesy Henry Sheldon Museum of Vermont History*

Outing at Taylor Park, Bank and Main Street, St. Albans, 1890. *Courtesy St. Albans Historical Society*

Winter Carnival, Burlington, late 1800s. *Photo courtesy Burlington photo file, UVM*

Middlebury High School base-ball team. Seated: Theodore Wells; Earl Bushman, Manger; Charles A. Adams, Standing: Arthur Parkhurst; ____Kimball; unidentified, Arthur James, Principal; Delmar Smith or Phillips; ____Cady; Harry Williams. *Courtesy Henry Sheldon Museum of Vermont History*

Exhibition Hall, formerly Addison City Courthouse, late 1800s.

Courtesy Henry Sheldon Museum of Vermont History

Hunting party in front of the Pierce House, Middlebury, October 1896. Those in the photo: Harry Williams, Ed Daniels, Cushing Hill, Jim Smith, John Higgins, DeWitt Walch, Arthur Coffin, Hub Potter. *Courtesy Henry Sheldon Museum of Vermont History*

Boating on Lake Champlain, circa 1910. In the photo: Theron Gregory, Daisy Bottom, Marianne Landon, Mark Chaffes, Frank Shackett, Charlotte Shackett, Alice Hayword, Carroll Bottom. *Courtesy Henry Sheldon Museum of Vermont History*

Vergennes High School boy's baseball team, circa 1905. *Courtesy Bixby Memorial Library*

Camp Martin, Milton, circa 1907. *Photo courtesy St. Albans Historical Society*

Lake Champlain from Battery Park, circa 1919. *Courtesy Burlington photo file, UVM*

First Winooski High School football team, early 1900s. *Courtesy L.L. McAllister collection, UVM*

Family picnic at the Essex Center Fair, 1916. *Courtesy Essex Historical Society, Harriett Powell Museum*

Crescent Beach, Burlington. *Courtesy Burlington photo file, UVM*

A crowd gathers after church at Queen City Park in Burlington, a booming resort in the early 1930s. In the mid-thirties the Queen City Park Hotel, owned by Charlie Lord, burned to the ground along with seven camps. It was never rebuilt and the era of tourism faded in Queen City Park. *Courtesy Burlington photo file, UVM*

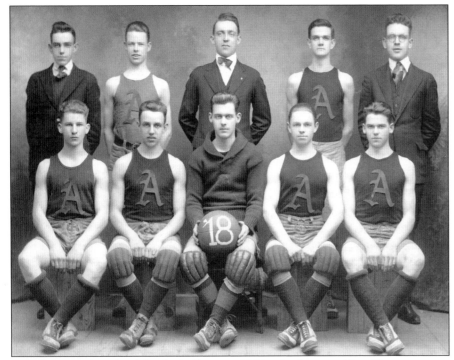

St. Albans High School basketball team, 1918. Back row: Tom Kennan, ____ Preston, Coach Doc. Crowley, Walter Jennings. Bottom row: Jessie Sunderland, Chandler Davis, Benjamin Center, Ralph Herrin, George Shannon. *Courtesy St. Albans Historical Society*

St. Albans High School, Vermont State Championship baseball team, 1922. Top row: B. Berrie, R. Alexander, E. Maloney, M. Godfrey, E. Willis, Coach J. Roach. Bottom row: C. Lambe, R. Lanuette, Captain P. Willis, I. Willett, D. Buckley and Perron was the mascot. *Courtesy St. Albans Historical Society*

Vergennes High School girls' basketball team, 1926-27. Back row: Kathleen Edwards, Katherine Tracy, Coach Wesley Smith, Lydia Gee, Margaret Gardner. Front row: Doris Barton, Freda Fishman (Captain), Dorothea Collins. *Courtesy Bixby Memorial Library*

St. Albans High School girls basketball team, 1924. *Courtesy St. Albans Historical Society*

Essex High School basketball team, 1933. *Courtesy Essex Historical Society, Harriett Powell Museum*

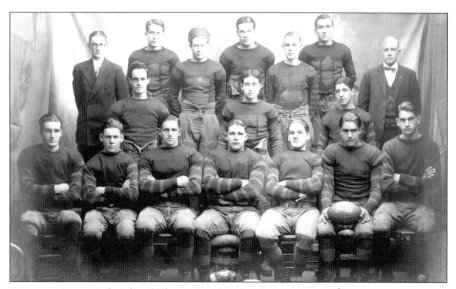

Vermont State High School Championship football team, 1926. H. Rugg, W. Bocash, M. Cochran, W. Sullivan, A. Collins, Captain S. Elias, N. Brown, E. Charron, H. Pelky, D. Lawrence, Manager A. Towhey, J. Davidson, C. Castonguay, J. Carter, H. Montgomery, R. McLeod and coach H.B. Dickinson. *Courtesy St. Albans Historical Society*

SBAA baseball team, Burlington, 1927. *Courtesy Burlington photo file, UVM*

PUBLIC SERVICE

Fort Ethan Allen was Vermont's largest military installation. Construction was completed in 1894 and legend has it that when Captain John G. Bourke of the Third Cavalry learned that his battalion was being transferred to Vermont, he and three other officers went to the officers' club "to wipe out our sorrows."

It was not as bad as they thought. In 1898, the Fort became a hub of activity in preparing men for the Spanish-American war. Fort Ethan Allen played an integral role in training Vermont's soldiers in WWI and WWII. It also was the staging area – and still is – for National Guard units.

Town life in the Valley's early years required volunteer service from its citizens: Police were volunteers, firemen were volunteers; post offices were often in someone's home or barn, judges had other jobs and those who ran the town government did so in their spare time.

In the late 1800s and early 1900s, the larger towns began to professionalize their staffs: Courts and police buildings were constructed; new fire stations housed the latest equipment and new, more permanent town and city halls were built.

Ft. Ethan Allen Artillery Range, Underhill, 1928. *Courtesy L.L. McAllister collection, UVM*

Badge worn by Middlebury Police Chief Clay Dickinson.

Courtesy Henry Sheldon Museum of Vermont History

First fire engine in St. Albans. Photo taken in Taylor Park, 1875. *Courtesy St. Albans Historical Society*

Clay Dickinson, Middlebury Chief of Police from 1876-1909. *Courtesy Henry Sheldon Museum of Vermont History*

Ferrisburgh Post Office and store, late 1800s. *Courtesy Bixby Memorial Library*

Addison County Court House was erected in 1796-98 on the brow of the hill, five or six rods north of the Chester Way residence. In 1816 it was removed to the site of the present Court House, and later removed to the Fair Grounds. The belfry was struck by lightening and removed. Afterwards it was called Floral Hall and torn down in 1940. *Courtesy Henry Sheldon Museum of Vermont History*

Town Hall, "Holley Hall," Bristol, circa 1900. *Courtesy Henry Sheldon Museum of Vermont History*

Burlington City Hall Park. *Courtesy Burlington photo file, UVM*

National Guard encampment, Burlington, 1904.

Courtesy Burlington photo file, UVM

Interior of the Winooski fire station, early 1900s. *Photo courtesy General Photo Collection, UVM*

The old white meeting house (Georgia Town Hall), 1902. It was built in 1802 and burned in 1953. *Courtesy Georgia Historical Society*

Volunteer firemen march in Vergennes during the Champlain Tercentenary Parade, 1909. *Courtesy Bixby Memorial Library*

Volunteer firemen race down the street during the Hub to Hub race, circa 1910. *Courtesy Bixby Memorial Library*

Essex Fire Department, circa 1910. *Courtesy Essex Historical Society, Harriett Powell Museum*

Construction of Burlington City Hall, 1926. *Courtesy Burlington photo file, UVM*

Construction of Burlington City Hall, 1926. *Courtesy Burlington photo file, UVM*

Huntington Post Office, circa 1910. *Courtesy Huntington Historical Community Trust*

St. Albans fire department, 1934. *Courtesy St. Albans Historical Society*

TRANSPORTATION

In the early years in Champlain Valley, transportation was difficult: roads were bad, passage over the mountains were bad, passage over the mountains difficult and time consuming and public transportation was confined to Lake Champlain and the rail lines.

The horse was the dominant means of locomotion in the 1800s. Horse-drawn buggies, wagons, sleds and coaches traveled the Valley's roads. In the cities, public transportation was by horse-drawn cars which were eventually replaced by electric trolleys and then, in the late 1920s, by buses.

In the late 1800s train travel became more prevalent; several of the region's railroads also owned and operated the ferries that criss-crossed Lake Champlain. In the Valley, the ferries brought people to work from their summer homes along the lake in Addison County.

The automobile made its appearance in the early 1900s, but they were more for pleasure than utility. Vermont's winters and mud season got the better of this new technology. Even as more of Vermont's roads were paved, car travel was slow until the 1960s when the interstates finally connected northern Vermont with the south.

From the late 1800s until the 1940s, train travel was extremely important to Vermont's economy: Vermont's products were hauled to the bigger cities to the south and Vermont's earliest tourists made their way north by way of the steam engine locomotive.

Horse-drawn buggy was one way to get around Hinesburg in the late 1800s. *Courtesy General Photo Collection, UVM*

Central Vermont Railroad's Engine No. 29, "Gov. Smith," circa 1883. *Courtesy General Photo Collection, UVM*

Rail road crew in front of Engine No. 7 at the engine house in St. Albans, circa 1880. *Courtesy St. Albans Historical Society*

Addison Hotel "bus," Middlebury, 1888. *Courtesy Henry Sheldon Museum of Vermont History*

First horse cars, Burlington, 1885. *Courtesy Burlington photo file, UVM*

Engine house, St. Albans, circa 1890. *Courtesy St. Albans Historical Society*

Opening of the Battell Stone Bridge, 1892. Included in the photo: Thad Chapman, mounted Marshal; M.T. Butterfield, driver of carriage; Mr. Henry L. Sheldon, Rev. Mr. Bidwell, George E. Hammond, a prominent sheep breeder; James M. Slade, a prominent lawyer and probate judge; Julius B. Benedict, a retired farmer; Thomas E. Wells, manager of Electric Light Company; Frank A. Bond, a prominent clothier; Joseph M. Burke, Town Clerk; Abram H. Langworthy, Water Department Manager. *Courtesy Henry Sheldon Museum of Vermont History*

Construction of the Battell Stone Bridge in Middlebury, 1891. *Courtesy Henry Sheldon Museum of Vermont History*

Battell Stone Bridge completed, circa 1892. *Courtesy Henry Sheldon Museum of Vermont History*

Trolley system going to the baseball park. St. Albans is playing Malone, New York, early 1900s. *Courtesy St. Albans Historical Society*

Georgia Highbridge construction, 1894. *Courtesy Georgia Historical Society*

The "Vermont" steamer on Lake Champlain, late 1800s. *Courtesy Bixby Memorial Library*

Georgia Highbridge construction crew, 1894. *Courtesy Georgia Historical Society*

Burlington Hotel stagecoach, late 1800s. *Courtesy Burlington photo file, UVM*

The "Reindeer" at Vergennes dock, late 1800s. *Courtesy Bixby Memorial Library*

Steamer "Reindeer" was one way to get around in the late 1800s. It sank at dock in 1902. *Courtesy Burlington photo file, UVM*

Burlington's Union Depot, late 1800s. *Courtesy Burlington photo file, UVM*

Herb Hall was the station agent at the East Georgia Depot, 1898.

Courtesy Georgia Historical Society

The "Victor" offered pleasure outings in the late 1800s. *Courtesy Bixby Memorial Library*

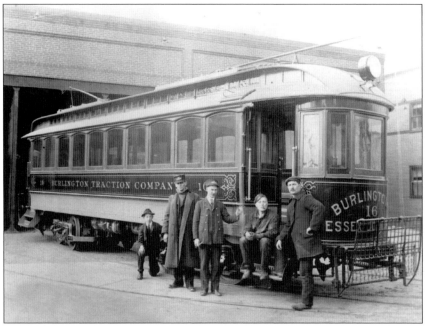

Burlington Traction company crew, early 1900s. *Courtesy Burlington photo file, UVM*

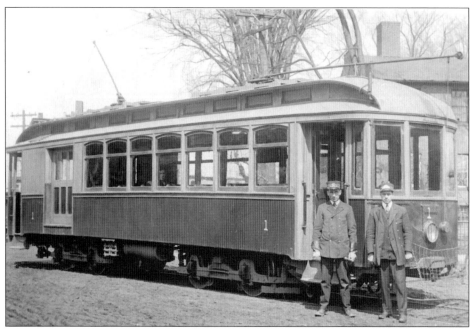

Trolley No. 1 and crew. *Courtesy Burlington photo file, UVM*

Opening of the St. Albans Street Railway, July 4, 1901. *Courtesy St. Albans Historical Society*

Ferry boat leaves Cedar Beach dock in Charlotte, early 1900s. *Courtesy General Photo Collection, UVM*

W & B Trolley, early 1900s. *Courtesy Burlington photo file, UVM*

St. Albans Street railway, early 1900s. *Courtesy St. Albans Historical Society*

Men who worked on the electric railway, St. Albans, circa 1905. *Courtesy St. Albans Historical Society*

Trolley No. 23 at Queen City Park, circa 1910. *Courtesy Burlington photo file, UVM*

Car rally in St. Albans, 1907. *Courtesy St. Albans Historical Society*

Central Vermont train nearing Burlington. *Courtesy General Photo Collection, UVM*

Central Vermont No. 319 locomotive, St. Albans, circa 1910. *Courtesy St. Albans Historical Society*

Early car in Burlington. *Photo courtesy L.L. McAllister collection, UVM*

Paving Main and West Allen streets, Winooski, 1920s. *Courtesy General Photo Collection, UVM*

Burlington Rapid Transit vehicles and drivers, 1926.

Courtesy Burlington photo file, UVM

Engine No. 49, Central Vermont Railroad, 1915. *Courtesy St. Albans Historical Society*

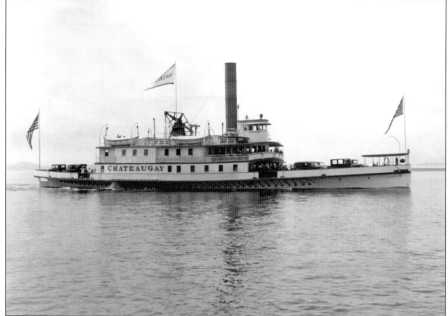

Ferry "Chateaugay" on Lake Champlain, 1925. *Courtesy L.L. McAllister collection, UVM*

Trolley on North Winooski Avenue, Burlington, October 1928. *Courtesy L.L. McAllister collection, UVM*

Preparing Pearl Street for paving, Burlington, October 27, 1928. *Courtesy L.L. McAllister collection, UVM*

Crowd gathers at Church Street, Burlington, to watch the burning of the last electric street car in Burlington, October 4, 1929. *Courtesy Burlington photo file, UVM*

Burning the last electric street car in Burlington, October 4, 1929. *Courtesy Burlington photo file, UVM*

Employees of the Burlington Rapid Transit Company, 1930. *Courtesy Burlington photo file, UVM*

Paving at the corner of North Street and North Avenue, Burlington, September 4, 1930. *Courtesy L.L. McAllister collection, UVM*

Burlington Municipal Airport under construction, June 21, 1935.
Courtesy L.L. McAllister collection, UVM

Burlington Municipal Airport. *Courtesy Burlington photo file, UVM*

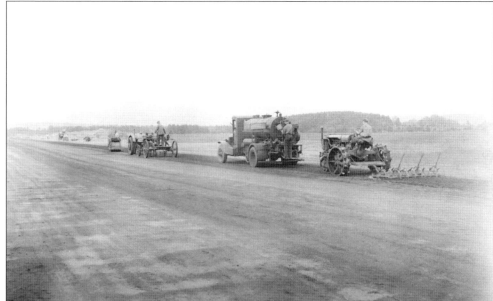

Burlington Municipal Airport under construction, June 21, 1935. *Courtesy L.L. McAllister collection, UVM*

Concrete ramp hangar and administration building at the Municipal Airport, Burlington, July 27, 1934. *Courtesy L.L. McAllister collection, UVM*

Burlington Street Department crew and equipment, 1930s *Courtesy L.L. McAllister collection, UVM*

Burlington Street Department crew and equipment April 17, 1937. *Courtesy L.L. McAllister collection, UVM*

Automobiles line up waiting for the Champlain Ferry, 1930s. *Courtesy L.L. McAllister collection, UVM*

DISASTERS

The rugged independent spirit of those who lived in the Valley was hardened by the many disasters that befell the state in the late 1800s and early 1900s. Fire, train wrecks, flu, floods, even a few hurricanes raised havoc with Vermonters' lives.

In the late 1800s, fire departments were strapped with what is, by today's standards, inefficient equipment and fire codes were non-existent. The Valley's cities – St. Albans, Burlington and Vergennes – experienced catastrophic fires that wiped out huge swaths of downtown buildings.

Bridge collapses, errant signals brought any number of train wrecks in the Valley, several were fatal.

In 1918, the Valley – and much of Vermont – was overwhelmed by an influenza that was virulent and quick: In one case, a woman on a train car went to bed apparently fine but was dead by morning. A total of 1,772 died in Vermont's worst human disaster.

The most devastating economic disaster hit the state in 1927 when torrents of rain fell non-stop on November 2, 3 and 4 in 1927. The rivers overflowed their banks by November 3 and the water did not subside for three days. More than 1,450 bridges were destroyed; 200 miles of road washed away; 690 farms were destroyed; 9,000 people left homeless and 84 killed, including the Vermont lieutenant governor.

Train wreck, Brooksville, August 30, 1889, crushed the railroad bridge. *Courtesy Henry Sheldon Museum of Vermont History*

Great fire in Burlington, 1888.
Courtesy Burlington photo file, UVM

Aftermath of the great
fire in Burlington, June
6, 1888. *Courtesy Burlington photo file, UVM*

Aftermath of the September 11, 1875 fire in Middlebury. *Courtesy Henry Sheldon Museum of Vermont History*

Aftermath of the September 11, 1875 fire in Middlebury. *Courtesy Henry Sheldon Museum of Vermont History*

Train wreck, Brooksville, August 30, 1889. *Courtesy Henry Sheldon Museum of Vermont History*

Main Street, Middlebury, after the November 1891 fire. *Courtesy Henry Sheldon Museum of Vermont History*

Aftermath of the November 1891 fire in Middlebury. This area was known as Merchants Row. *Courtesy Henry Sheldon Museum of Vermont History*

St. Albans was plagued with a series of fires in the second half of the nineteenth century. After large fires in 1868 and again in 1871, the city implemented underground water service for the central business district, fed by a hill-side reservoir above the town. The worst fire in the town's history occurred in 1895 and consumed nearly a quarter of the city center destroying over 100 structures in three square blocks. *Courtesy St. Albans Historical Society*

Industrial School fire in the administration building, Vergennes, 1914. *Courtesy Bixby Memorial Library*

Ruins of Hibbard Block, after the November 4, 1911 fire in Burlington. *Courtesy Burlington photo file, UVM*

Aftermath of the St. Albans fire, 1895. *Courtesy St. Albans Historical Society*

Aftermath of the 1927 flood, Proctor. *Courtesy Henry Sheldon Museum of Vermont History*

Aftermath of the 1927 flood, Proctor. *Courtesy Henry Sheldon Museum of Vermont History*

Aftermath of the 1927 flood, Proctor. *Courtesy Henry Sheldon Museum of Vermont History*

Floodwaters take out a bridge in Winooski, 1927. *Photo courtesy General Photo Collection, UVM*

High water in a residential area, East Middlebury, 1937 flood. *Courtesy Henry Sheldon Museum of Vermont History*

Aftermath of the 1927 flood, Waterbury. *Courtesy Henry Sheldon Museum of Vermont History*

Aftermath of the November 1927 flood, East Middlebury. *Courtesy Henry Sheldon Museum of Vermont History*

Sherwood Hotel fire, February 3, 1937. *Courtesy Burlington photo file, UVM*

CELEBRATION

Vermonters love a good parade. And in the early years of Champlain Valley, there was plenty to celebrate. On Oct. 12, 1899, Montpelier was jammed with celebrants for Dewey Day, an honor for Adm. George Dewey, a Montpelier native and Spanish-American War hero. The only problem was Dewey hated crowds.

A decade later in July 1909, towns and cities along the Lake celebrated the tercentenary, the 300th anniversary of Samuel de Champlain's discovery of the lake that bears his name. In Burlington, President William Taft and British Ambassador James Bryce arrived for the festivities via the Ticonderoga.

Bryce, in his speech to the throng, urged Vermonters to protect their mountains and lakes "as the place in which relive will have to be sought from the constantly growing strain of our modern life."

Fourth of July, centennials, "Old Home Week," dedications, Memorial Day, Armistice Day, even Preparedness Day, Vermonters always have found a way to march to music with a flag and a horse and a smile.

Champlain Tercentenary Parade in Vergennes, July 3, 1909. *Courtesy Bixby Memorial Library*

Parade down Main Street, St. Albans, 1800s. *Courtesy St. Albans Historical Society*

Unidentified parade down Church Street, Burlington, late 1800s. *Courtesy Burlington photo file, UVM*

Republican First Voters Club on Bank Street at Taylor Park, St. Albans, 1893. *Courtesy St. Albans Historical Society*

Centennial Celebration, Vergennes, 1866 marking the 100-year anniversary of the first settlement by Donald McIntosh. The city was incorporated in 1788. The sign was made by the ladies of Vergennes. There were 2,000 in attendance. *Courtesy Bixby Memorial Library*

Mrs. Twigg's carriage in front of her home on High Street, St. Albans, during the celebration of "Old Home Week" in 1898. *Courtesy St. Albans Historical Society*

Dedication of the Ethan Allen Tower, Burlington, August 16, 1905. *Courtesy Burlington photo file, UVM*

Vergennes all decked out for the Champlain Tercentenary celebration by John Alden, 1909. Arches were built out of wooden frames and covered with unbleached muslin. Harry Herrick, owner of the shoe store helped with the decorations. *Courtesy Bixby Memorial Library*

Champlain Tercentenary Celebration in Burlington, 1909. *Courtesy Burlington photo file, UVM*

Champlain Tercentenary Parade in Vergennes, July 3, 1909.
Courtesy Bixby Memorial Library

Parade down Main Street, Vergennes, circa 1910. *Courtesy Bixby Memorial Library*

Marching down a Vergennes street during the Macdonough Centennial Parade, 1914. *Courtesy Bixby Memorial Library*

Float in the 150th anniversary celebration in Jericho, 1913. *Courtesy Clinton M. Russell, Jr. and Barbara Mudgett-Russell*

Ralph Oscar Mudgett's hardware store float in a Memorial Day Parade, Essex Junction, 1912. *Courtesy Essex Community Historical Soceity, Harriet Powell Museum*

Float in the 150th anniversary celebration in Jericho, 1913. *Courtesy Clinton M. Russell, Jr. and Barbara Mudgett-Russell*

Lorraine (Jaques) Jones and Barbara Spaulding all dressed up for the Fourth of July parade, Huntington. *Courtesy Huntington Historical Community Trust, Lorraine Jones collection*

Preparedness Parade on Main Street, Burlington, May 19, 1917. *Courtesy Burlington photo file, UVM*

Armistice Day Parade on Main Street, Burlington, November, 1918. *Courtesy Burlington photo file, UVM*